D1500023

WEST OF CHILDHOOD

Poems 1950–1965

Isabella Gardner

WEST OF
CHILDHOOD

Poems 1950–1965

HOUGHTON MIFFLIN COMPANY BOSTON
THE RIVERSIDE PRESS CAMBRIDGE
1965

West of Childhood includes all of the poems that appeared in *Birthdays from the Ocean* (Houghton Mifflin Company, 1955). Copyright 1951, 1952, 1953, 1954, 1955 by Isabella Gardner McCormick. The poems published in *The Looking Glass* (The University of Chicago Press, 1961) are reprinted here by kind permission of The University of Chicago Press. © 1961 by The University of Chicago.

The poems in this volume first appeared in the following journals:

Accent: The Sloth, Reveille for a Rockinghorse Winner. *The Atlantic Monthly:* To Thoreau on Rereading Walden, Canzonetta, Summer Remembered. *Beloit Poetry Journal:* Summers Ago. *Botteghe Oscure:* Of Flesh and Bone. *Chicago Choice:* A Part of the Dark. *Chicago Magazine:* West of Childhood. *Chicago Review:* Saloon Suite, Zei Gesund. *Encounter:* This Room Is Full of Clocks. *Furioso:* Homo Gratia Artis. *The Hudson Review:* Cock-a-Hoop, The Only Relic, Letter from Slough Pond. *The Kenyon Review:* The Minotaur, Timeo. *The Minnesota Review:* The Searchlight, A Loud Song, Mother. *Mutiny:* Little Rock Arkansas 1957, In Memory of Lemuel Ayers. *New Orleans Poetry Journal:* Gimboling, Abraham and Isaac. *The New Republic:* Bedtime Story, Mathematics of Encounter. *New World Writing:* Lines to a Seagreen Lover. *The New Yorker:* In the Museum, The Compleat Anglers, The Masked Shrew, At a Summer Hotel. *The Paris Review:* Children Are Game. *Partisan Review:* That "Craning of the Neck." *Poetry: A Magazine of Verse:* Cowardice, The Panic Vine, The Milkman, Cadenza, Three Rings or Five Rings, Fall in Massachusetts, It Rained Last Night, Southwest of True North, The Widow's Yard, And Now No Breath at All, A Word From the Piazza del Limbo. *Poetry Northwest:* Roundelay. *Prairie Schooner:* Mea Culpa. *The Sewanee Review:* At the Zoo, When in Rome, Summer Evening, Nightmare, The Looking Glass. *The Texas Quarterly:* Writing Poetry, Not at All What One Is Used to. *The Yale Literary Magazine:* When a Warlock Dies.

To Allen

"Love consists in this: that two solitudes
protect and touch, and greet each other."

RAINER MARIA RILKE

Contents

I

II

III

VI

I

Letter from Slough Pond

Here where you left me alone
the soft wind sighs through my wishbone
the sun is lapping at my flesh
I couple with the ripples of the fresh
pond water I am rolled by the roiling sea.
Love, in our wide bed, do you lie lonely?
The spoon of longing stirs my marrow
and I thank God this bed is narrow.

To Thoreau on Rereading Walden

"I long ago lost a hound, a bay horse, and a turtle-dove."

"There too, as everywhere I sometimes expected the visitor who never comes."   HENRY THOREAU

Your passion was ever plural, apart
from that one twig ("the twig") you never found.
Herds of birds and fishes, stars in droves
received your taut and tender gaze
but gills beaks planets can't reciprocate
and gratefully you prayed their praise.
You loved the faces in the fire, Thoreau,
the goldgreen pickerel, the huddling snow.
I too love these, and O love you, fierceheart,
and yet were you, like Lazarus, to rise,
you would look everywhere but in my eyes.
You'd hear the loud spring ice the greening ground,
but not the caller knocking at your gate
nor the nickering in your maple groves
nor the howling for home of the hound.
You did not listen to the turtle-dove
(singular bird) sing on your lintel: LOVE
And now no visitor will come to crowd
Your peace. You have dried safely in your shroud.

At a Summer Hotel

FOR MY DAUGHTER,
ROSE VAN KIRK

I am here with my beautiful bountiful womanful child
to be soothed by the sea not roused by these roses roving wild.
My girl is gold in the sun and bold in the dazzling water,
she drowses on the blond sand and in the daisy fields my
    daughter
dreams. Uneasy in the drafty shade I rock on the veranda
reminded of Europa Persephone Miranda.

On Looking in the Looking Glass

You small embattled eyes dispute a face
that middle-aging sags and creases.
Besieged, your eyes protest and plead,
your wild little eyes are bright, and bleed.

And now in an instant's blink my stare
seizes in your beleaguered glare
the pristine gaze the blown-glass stance
of your once
total innocence.
I see and dare the child you were.

And for a wink's lasting. There
Now in your blistered eyes dazzles the flare
of Youth with years and love to swear
the kindling enkindled fire
heedless and sheer . . .
I see and fear the girl you were.

And now for a tic's lending, Now for the stint
of a second's fission I light to the glint
of your Daemon, that familiar whom you stint
so prodigally. Shunting, shan't-
ing, wincing fabricant
I see the maker that you want
and aren't.

And now just now I closed your eyes
your infant ancient naked eyes.
Gaze glare and flare and glint are buried by
my neutral eye-
lids. These island citadels are now surrendered
and with imagination's eye I see you dead.

The Masked Shrew

. . . The Masked Shrew . . . approximately one year
of fastpaced gluttonous life.   LIFE MAGAZINE

A penny is heavier than the shrew,
dim-eyed and weaker than a worm
this smallest mammal, cannoned by a sudden noise,
lies down and dies.
No furnace gluttons fiercer than the shrew
devouring daily with relentless appetite
four times her inchling body's weight.
More extravagant than the hummingbird's the shrew's
heart beats per minute twice four hundred times.
If foodless for six hours she is dead.
The helpless, hungry, nervous shrew
lives for a year of hurly-burly
and dies intolerably early.

Of Flesh and Bone

Child and girl each morning summer winter or dismay
my eyes saw waterfalls my ears heard madrigals I ta-
sted strawberries touched moss smelt hay and roses, and through
 the blue
the bright sky I with my first and once-love flew.
Willow-boned sun-marrowed and air-skinned,
sea-water in my veins, I drank wine and the southwest wind.
The noun death and the verb to die were exiled from my
vocabulary, and when the salty boys and sun-burned girls I
mooned with on the honeysuckled porch through locust-
loud and sigh-soft summer nights did speculate upon the dispo-
 sition of my dust
I said to them I am a girl of flesh and bone, my shift's no
 shroud,
and d-e-a-t-h is the word I do not say out loud.
That is the word I said that I will not admit.
(I had read of a fatal Irish ghost named IT
who reeked corruption and whose gaze was potent as the
 basilisk,
and IT became my parlor slang for the noun I dared not risk)
The salty boys bugled desire to die at thirty-five
and the girls harped a lust to be buried, not old maimed and
 alive.
I vowed that eyeless earless loinless lonely,
I would refuse to die; that even if only
one sense was left me, touch or smell or taste,

I would choose to live; that in a sewer of waste
a thicket of pain a mountain of fear or the sea-
wrack of sorrow I would beg, steal, and betray to be.
Girl and child my nightmare was the ceasing,
not the attendant pinch and panic, but the releasing
of the I. Now that my blood's a sweeter blend,
now that my bones are bones and do not bend
now that my skin is dressed, what sucks my marrow
is not the final act of IT but the engagement some tomorrow.
The certainty, in spite of locking doors and looking in the
    closets, that IT may wait
around That corner, under an unfamiliar bed, or through next
    summer's gate.
The meeting of ITS gaze in a sick second's shock of infinite
    danger
and then the slow or sudden but unrefusable embrace and the
    intolerable anger.
I am not faith-less but with those who see no future in eternity
    I do agree,
no paradise and no inferno will resolve the coming nothingness
    of me.
Mice and lions also die but God spared beasts our "knowing
    that we know"
today and yesterday, tomorrow, creeds and crimes ago.

Now mornings are still miracles and my dear now-love is my
    true
love and we fly we fly . . . O the sky was never once so bright
    and blue
and I still wish to live with living's theft-
ing and assault if even one sense will be left,

but to escape the meals and miles of waiting
I might elect the hour of my negating
and sleep peacefully to death some winter night,
cold finally to morning and to mourners and to fright.
Still, flesh and bone is wilful, and this knowledge is dead-certain
and my horror,
that I shall not close my eyes when ITS eyes stare out of mine
in every mirror.

The Milkman

The door was bolted and the windows of my porch
were screened to keep invaders out, the mesh of rust-
proof wire sieved the elements. Did my throat parch
then sat I at my table there and ate with lust
most chaste, the raw red apples; juice, flesh, rind and core.

One still and summer noon while dining in the sun
I was poulticing my thirst with apples, slaking care,
when suddenly I felt a whir of dread. Soon, soon,
stiff as a bone, I listened for the Milkman's tread.
I heard him softly bang the door of the huge truck
and then his boots besieged my private yard. I tried
to keep my eyes speared to the table, but the suck
of apprehension milked my force. At last he mounted
my backstairs, climbed to the top, and there he stood still
outside the bolted door. The sun's color fainted.
I felt the horror of his quiet melt me, steal
into my sockets, and seduce me to him from
my dinner. His hand clung round the latch like rubber.
I felt him ooze against the screen and shake the frame.
I had to slide the bolt; and thus I was the robber
of my porch. Breathing smiling shape of fright,
the Milkman made his entrance; insistent donor,
he held in soft bleached hands the bottled sterile fruit,
and gave me this fatal, this apostate dinner.
Now in winter I have retreated from the porch

into the house and the once red apples rot where
I left them on the table. Now if my throat parch
for fruit the Milkman brings a quart for my despair.

Cadenza

Conjure away the blue and the dim and the dark cloths
I am no longer in the night or in the half light
I want a shout of white and an aria of fire
and a paean of green and a coral carillon
not Cinderella's slippers not the Emperor's new clothes
not the skull behind the flower but the bone that is the rose.

II

The Widow's Yard

"Snails lead slow idyllic lives . . ."
The rose and the laurel leaves
in the raw young widow's yard
were littered with silver. Hard-
ly a leaf lacked the decimal scale
of the self of a snail. Frail
in friendship I observed with care
these creatures (meaning to spare
the widow's vulnerable eyes
the hurting pity in my gaze).

Snails, I said, are tender skinned.
Excess in nature . . . sun rain wind
are killers. To save themselves
snails shrink to shelter in their shells
where they wait safe and patient
until the elements are gent-
ler. And do they not have other foes?
the widow asked. Turtles crows
foxes rats, I replied, and canned
heat that picnickers aband-
on. Also parasites invade
their flesh and alien eggs are laid
inside their skins. Their mating
too is perilous. The meeting
turns their faces blue with bliss

17

and consummation of this
absolute embrace is so
extravagantly slow
in coming that love begun
at dawn may end in fatal sun.
The widow told me that her
husband knew snails' ways and his garden had been Eden for them. He
said the timid snail could lift three
times his weight straight up and haul
a wagon toy loaded with a whole
two hundred times his body's burden.
Then as we left the garden
she said that at the first faint chill
the first premonition of fall
the snails go straight to earth . . . excrete
the lime with which they then secrete
the opening in their shells . . . and wait for spring.
It is those little doors which sing,
she said, when they are boiled.
She smiled at me when I recoiled.

The Last Trump

You suddenly squeak breathlessly like a squeezed rubber toy
you scream and scrabble in my kitchen, I am paralyzed.
You doomed freak of black and white you with your cockaded
 soul
self-freed self-housed and now self-trapped behind the hunching
 white
appliances that loom and glitter on the lunch-stained wall.
The reasoned breach between these units will not admit the
 most starved arm
or straining finger, no broom nor torch can bruise or burn or
 succor you
charity's green cheese is scattered on the waxed inlaid linoleum
(in death you smell the vinegared sponge) pragmatic mouse
 afraid to wait
for loaves and fishes, frightened to inch within a mouse-length
 of the bait
afraid to sleep inside the box contrived for you a grocer's carton
rag-padded, screened, stocked with a doll's dish of water and
 the choicest crumbs
to nourish you. Did you find freedom behind the stove icebox
 and sink?
Untemptable mouse, soon dead, and no one nothing can remove
 your stink
no light invade your coffin to focus on your rank ironic corpse

no dialectic can deny you. Your turd your bones your crucial
  shriek
will curd the lion's hollandaise, will thicken and goose the
  children's milk.

Southwest of True North

Displaced by sandy distances
from tide and time and season,
detached from cadenced air and ballad
wind, from root and rime and reason;
shored where scarce water is voiceless
and ceaseless birds sing brashly out
of tune, beached in an alien landscape
a huge montage of drought
an impersonal district devoid of felicity
where neither the consonance of harmony
nor the complicity
of dissonance exists I loom and blunder
in a blast-bright land not by the grace
of God and suns evolved but conjured into ominous being.
In this assembled place
where matter hums with coiled intent
autonomous vitality
and no mineral vegetable animal or element
pertains to another; where no thing ripens or
decays, where life is reduced to existence
and existence to decor,
I find the birds especially intolerable.

These insolent incessant birds
loud bland indifferent feathered herds

as unrelated to this desert as the rocks and sand
as the cactus, creeks, creatures, weather, wind, and
I, yet breeding being dying in these regions
that I visit with a reaching eye; these gaudy legions
bold and practical as tourists,
flaunting detachment, wagging their
barnyard tails at my shocked seeking stare
twanging and harping as though I were not here
(as if to say
Don't bother with the salt tweak our tailfeathers any day . . .)
cocking a vulgar beak at me and my devotions
my barefoot Audubon–Saint Francis notions.

I cannot seduce these birds with love and a bread crumb,
nor startle them,
nor silently and undiscovered come
upon a thicket-full
to listen, concealed by my own care
and skill and will while they are singing
and unaware.
Never never can I approach them found
and finding to hear full frolic voices mute
to not a decibel of sound
till the perilous pause dissolving
resolves to a decimal dazzle of scale
a sheer precarious fluting of greeting
a flickering miracled carol of Hail.

North of this neighborhood I have been quickened by such
        canticles.
I am no guest

of these unbirdly birds. They are not disposed to manifest
concern with my immediacy. There is no benison or ban
from them to me. As though invisible I am not even an
intruder, am neither enemy nor friend,
have no identity.
Aroint thee birds
though hexed I am not your familiar. Nonentity,
I need a fang, a tusk, a talon, a bellow, a hiss, a roar
to un-bewitch me, one methodical
rattlesnake, an eager dinosaur,
an uncorrupted scorpion, a dedicated flea,
some single indigenous monster apt to acknowledge me.
Unlikely fantasy.
Not even the essence of evil is unalloyed
in this indecent territory,
the temper of the wildest beast is cloyed
to brisk neutrality.
No mythic wings whir down this shallow sky
to conquer these chimeric ciphers that neither listen nor reply.
I had expected residual souls in the local birds even at this
compass point. But environment is a factor difficult to alter
or dismiss.

> Birds in a vulnerable land
> where there is sea to salt the sand
> I rut, and roost, and rot, and sing,
> occasionally on the wing.

The Sloth

Body very hairy, tenacious of life.
CARL LINNAEUS (1707-1778)

Two centuries ago Linnaeus said "noise frightful, tears pitiful"
   of you,
bungled one. Arm over hairy arm you travel having no heels
to take to on your unsoled feet, no hole to hide in, and no way
   to fight.
Doomed to the trees, "good food for many," your one safety
   is in flight.

Today the scarce and lonely sloth, obedient prisoner in space,
astonished by perpetual pain looks askingly into my face
and hangs by legs and arms to life inexorably upside down
under branches in the zoo or in the subway under town.

Part of the Darkness

I had thought of the bear in his lair as fiercely free, feasting
    on honey and wildwood fruits;
I had imagined a forest lunge, regretting the circus shuffle and
    the zoo's proscribed pursuits.
Last summer I took books and children to Wisconsin's Great
    North woods. We drove
one night through miles of pines and rainy darkness to a garbage
    grove
that burgeoned broken crates and bulging paper bags and
    emptied cans of beer,
to watch for native bears, who local guides had told us,
    scavenged there.
After parking behind three other cars (leaving our headlights on
    but dim)
We stumbled over soggy moss to join the families blinking on
    the rim
of mounded refuse bounded east north and west by the forest.
The parents hushed and warned their pushing children each of
    whom struggled to stand nearest
the arena, and presently part of the darkness humped away
    from the foliage and lumbered bear-shaped
toward the heaping spoilage. It trundled into the litter while
    we gaped,
and for an instant it gaped too, bear-faced, but not a tooth was
    bared. It grovelled
carefully while tin cans clattered and tense tourists tittered.

Painstakingly it nosed and ravelled
rinds and husks and parings, the used and the refused; bear-
skinned and doggedly explored
the second-hand remains while headlights glared and flashlights
stared and shamed bored
children booed, wishing aloud that it would trudge away so
they might read its tracks.
They hoped to find an as yet unclassified spoor, certain that no
authentic bear would turn his back
upon the delicacies of his own domain to flounder where mere
housewives' leavings rot.
I also was reluctant to concede that there is no wild honey in
the forest and no forest in the bear.
Bereaved, we started home, leaving that animal there.

At the Zoo

O the phoenix is gone and the unicorn
and the Chinese Nightingale.
No white whale blows
nor Persian rose,
the buffalo is robe and dust.

I have a headlong leaping lust
for zig and zag and hues and cries,
for the paradox of the musky ox
and the mute giraffe's embarrassed eyes.

One should not (in this zoo) throw down a glove.
It is the bars that shame a zebra out of love
and flinch the tender faces of giraffes
who stick their necks out and are good for laughs.
The beautiful the gentle the enraged
the strange the pitiful are shooed and caged
the preying cats and the shy kine who browse
on treetops. Peanuts are not thrown to cows.

If the buffalo quicken in his hide
and the phoenix rise and the virgin bride
lie with the unicorn
Roland's horn and Omar's rose and Moby Dick will blow
and every piper will be pied and cages will be never,
giraffes will wink and zebras prink and spring come on forever.

Reveille for a Rockinghorse Poet

Don't "trot trot to Bost-
on" child, gallop to Bordeaux.
Not every bell change has been rung
Nor every monster seen.
Hunt the Whale the Grail the Fleece
Kiss the cockatrice in Greece.

Don't "trot trot to market," child. Canter through Cockaigne.
Singlefoot to Samarkand and steeplechase in Spain
though far away translates to mean
(in the Zulu tongue)
"That place where someone cries out O
mother I am lost."

Bedtime Story

"Here is a candle to light you to bed
here comes the chopper to chop off your head"

That princeling bland with dapper smiles for daylit danger,
that dauphin gay as a dolphin at high noon,
in the purring night, pawed by the furry darkness,
howls mutely at the looming loneliness.

In his cold comfortable cage (unguarded)
bulging with beasts, pulsing with strangers,
in a ferocity of silence, it is his own
soft breath that pads and pants and pauses.

Bereaved and unbelieved, beset, be-nighted,
wincing from the awaited and insupportable pounce,
his little tender burrowing bones
bury him to bed.
    No lance no bow of burning gold
    No ewe no shepherd and no fold
    No jerkin of green nor coat of mail, no grace nor grail
    Can celebrate or succour him. Fearful and frail
that trembling desolate and dear prince cringes on his cot
while down unending corridors behind an arras (innocent and
    not
unarrogant with unicorns) the dauntless King and Queen
waltz sumptuously to sleep.

Abraham and Isaac

"Behold the fire and the wood but where is the lamb
for the burnt offering?" said little Isaac trembling.
"God will provide," said Abraham.

> Fathers of Isaacs cease dissembling.
> Will every thicket yield a ram?

III

"Wo o Wo ist der Ort?"

RILKE

Three Rings or Five Rings

Three rings or five rings no one would look for him in the
    main tent.
Where is the tendon and the soul to walk a rope
or even the tall cruelty to crack a whip
guts to heel-hang from a bar catch comrades from a dangled
    strand
brass to blare a horn, grace to crowd-wise tap music from the
    band?
He has not the muscled wit to juggle nor the accident
of beauty blood-rare and wild to prowl stage center in a cage.
Focused men who shove with pride sell cotton candy in the
    stands.
The calloused cautious roustabout takes pains with quick bare
    hands.
Punctual innocence sweeps the tanbark in between the acts
and humilty leaps venerant to horses' schooled gay backs.

Clowns explode in pity and love (whimpers embarrass children
    into rage).
He is not caparisoned for the main tent. In the side-show
    mightily
he flirts adjusting his mock-mournful smile while cynically he
    poses there
cosily naked as though in his own parlor, a near hermaphrodite,
not a genuine freak but reason enough for our despair.

Mea Culpa

I do not love thee, Doctor Fell
The reason why I cannot tell
But this one thing I know full well
I do not love thee, Dr. Fell

The plane rose loudly and rammed west
while I, as usual afraid, rejoiced
that the stranger beside me hid
the window's terrible view of our toy
enormous tinkered wing tilting
and shuddering out there
in the middle of the air.

I looked at the man by my side
and saw one eye, cheek, ear, and hearing aid.
His tears fell out the eye and down the cheek.
Turning his head he fused his spilling gaze
to mine and begging angrily he said
"I am a surgeon hired to patch
the almost dead alive
but Doctor Fell will not arrive.

He is expected; and further
he is expected by the families
of the dying, who pay his monstrous fee
and fare, to be God Almighty's cousin . . .
whereas, clearly, I am not even
on time, lady, not even perhaps in
time, because a flight was cancelled." Knowing
him deaf I loudly cried

him grace, yelling, "You tried . . .
and they will know that you tried."

He mentioned trains and that they run on time
and that perhaps the waiting dying man
had died. "Yes, I am a surgeon," he said
softly, "but I had rather peddle used
cars to buy my beer. I am tired I
am tired of this frightful trust when I
confront and cut a bleeding carcass."
Touching his hand I blared
that the very FACT that he cared . . .

"Care, care," he said as tears still slid
from his eyes, "can't you see I am not there?"
Abruptly he pulled a silver pill-box
from his pocket, and showing me his hands
and how they shook, he said, "I take a pill
at intervals to make my hands belong
and if I time the taking perfectly
these hands behave; they are golden, lady,
not one qualm or quiver in these
fingers, in these wrists, this heart,
or any other part."

I thought but could not bellow, yes, you care,
but the choice was yours; you made it leniently.
Your tears and pills and knives, my glib compassion
and my cadenced cant, these bleeding hearts
that blossom on our sleeves will not enlarge the
spirit, Doctor, nor reduce the spleen. We

must commit the act of caring before
indulging in elegiac tears. Our bills and
visits must be paid, our letters written,
our departures and arrivals made on time.
Trusting your weather eye
You assumed that plane would fly.

"Please forgive me that I have no comfort
for you" . . . I spoke out loud, but, not, it seemed,
quite loud enough, for he paid no heed, and
kneading his hands, remained silent until
our plane landed. I wished then to will him
well, but under the circumstances,
a resonant Good Luck struck me as flippant,
and a shouted Good-bye redundant.

Saloon Suite

I. Accordion and Harmonica
                (Accordion)   Waltz
The red balloon will collapse, my sweet
The snowman will melt in the sun
The daffodil dries on the hill
                                AND
the kite blows away out of sight
But the hurdy the gurdy still giddies the street
                and lilacs are BLOO-
                      ming in Kew
and the dancing the dancing
the rhyming romancing
will never no never be done.

                (Harmonica)   Jig
Murphy and company jig with Cohen
Shicker vie a Goy
Sing your slainthe landsmen
Lhude sing Lockheim
Joy and joy and joy
AND
Paesani   Please It's time

NOTE: This poem was written after hearing the "Third Man
      Theme," which should be kept in mind while reading
      Part II. "Shicker vie a Goy" is Yiddish for "drunk like
      a gentile," "Slainthe" is the Gaelic equivalent of "Here's
      to you," and "Lockheim" is Yiddish for "slainthe." "Lands-
      men" is Yiddish for "fellow townsmen."

II. Zither   Tango
Loving you   Love   loving you
the least leaf
the least last lone-est leaf
redder is, red red   is redder
redder than   that maple grove
in fall   in fall in fall
                          and in
and in the spring   in the spring
the youngest and the littlest leaf
                  is green
a greener green a greenest green ah greener than
a willow tree
                  in May
in May in May
I love you, love you love   you far-
ther, than the farthest foam in
furthest most for ever wake of sea-
lost shallop
and more particularly Love,   than
the look!   look looked-for shell than
the sought-found-shell than
the small and the whole shell's
sweet scallop.
Lost love-lost   love-lost
I am lost Love I am lost love-lost
Love lost.
Sail me sail me home
Sail me sail me sail me home
My sailor   sail me sail me HOME

Reef me   steer me.   Navigate me
home   home   home   home
home.

Lines to a Seagreen Lover

My lover never danced with me
Not minuet nor sarabande
We walked (embracing) on the sand

My lover never swam with me
We waded to our ankle bones
And winced and shivered on the stones

My lover never flew with me
We stared at sea birds slicing space
And cried What freedom Look what grace

I wish my love had lain with me
Not on the sand beside the sea
But under my ailanthus tree

Mathematics of Encounter

Two never-ever-will-be lovers each
thatched in a thicket of one-
liness, huddled in onlyhood,
reach eye to perilous eye and contract
in an absolute gaze, in a clasping
of I's, a wedding. In that (ah marginal)
marrying of marrows, flesh blooms and bells,
blood shimmers and arrows, bones melt
and meld, loins lock.
In that look's-lasting love is resolved
to one-plus-one, dissolved again to two, these two absolved,
and the equation solved.

The Compleat Anglers

Wing fin and wrist bend wishfully
to cadences of summer noon
and courting lovers cast their bait
into the laden air of love.

The deft rod waits the still stream stirs
and mute gills tremble to the lure,
the lovers' taut hands listen to
soft nimble arias of love.

A ridden hawk screams like a cat
as hook is caught as mouth is reamed
as reeling lovers play their catch
through foaming areas of love.

Summer Evening

The salmon west leapt soft, spawned wild to sunset,
and the poaching lovers stood heron-still in the foam
of the orchard, baited to catch some sound of home,
while no dog barked and no door slammed and no child shouted.
But poplar leaves clashed like cymbals in the thin wind that
    blew
and at last the moon boomed out of the apple-tree and the two
lovers dove into the amorous dusk
and swam like swans through the clamorous air.

Gimboling

Nimble as dolphins to
dive leap and gimble, sleek, supple
as ripples to slip round each other to
wander and fondle on under and into
the seeking and coupling and swarming of water
compliant as sea-plants to bend with the tide
unfolding and folding to frond and to flower
a winding and twining to melt and to merge
to rock upon billowing founder in surf
and a fathom's down drowning before the sweet waking
the floating ashore into sleep and to morning.

The Searchlight

from an anti-aircraft battery

In smug delight we swaggered through the park
and arrogant pressed arm and knee and thigh.
We could not see the others in the dark.
We stopped and peered up at the moonless sky
and at grey bushes and the bristling grass
You in your Sunday suit, I in my pleated gown,
deliberately we stooped (brim-full of grace,
each brandied each rare-steaked) and laid us down.

We lay together in that urban grove
an ocean from the men engaged to die.
As we embraced a distant armoured eye
aroused our dusk with purposed light, a grave
rehearsal for another night. The field
bloomed lovers, dined and blind and target-heeled.

Roundelay

A blood-red bird with one green eye
and one gilt wing is hanging high.
Slung by the neck on a Christmas tree
dangling there in the tinsel he
is not about to sing for me.

The tree it trembles, the glass gauds swing
like that bird with his one gilt wing
who bows his beak, whose one eye glows
as back and forth and round he goes
to grace notes and arpeggios.

Cock-a-Hoop

How struts my love my cavalier
How crows he like a chanticleer
How softly I am spurred my dear;
Our bed is feathered with desire
And this yard safe from fox and fire.
But spurless on the dunghill, dead,
The soldier's blood is rooster red,
His seed is spent and no hen fed,
Alas no chick of this sweet cock
Will speak for Christ at dawn o'clock.

IV

"Je est un autre"

RIMBAUD

"Le moi est haissable"

PASCAL

In the Museum

Small and emptied woman you lie here a thousand years dead
your hands on your diminished loins flat in this final bed
teeth jutting from your unwound head your spiced bones black
   and dried,
who knew you and kissed you and kept you and wept when
   you died;
died you young had you grace? Risus sardonicus replied.
Then quick I seized my husband's hand while he stared at his
   bride.

The Only Relic

Hunting for coppers of Alaskan braves
in a forest of totem poles and graves
I found a skull no bigger than my eye,
greenish white, light as breath, and the only
relic there. I wondered who had to die
leaving just a bony scream and lonely
holes where eyelids blinked and no arms no loins.

Back home (with no beads no feathers no coins)
I hid the skull in a blue box with rings
I never wear these days and jagged things
crystal and turquoise I shall never mend
and moonstone cuff-links that I mean to send
back. The delicate anguished rigid shout
is still intact. But I shall take it out
now, place it on the mantelpiece, and wait
till children hide the fragments in the grate.

When in Rome . . .

It seemed a fine day for a canter.

The lady riding through the cattle corn
swung her right leg around the saddle horn
convinced the dun cow pony was a jennet
bell bridled flower wreathed and white as rennet.
The lady's breeches belled to a blue velvet habit featly
full; plumes brushed her cheek, her tasseled gloves moved neatly
through the ribboned reins. Dismounting by a willow tree
hung with mistletoe she sat upon the sandy sward,
gently expecting an encounter:
while around her the immodest birds exclaimed discordantly
reminding the still lady of her plight.

Alas too seasoned for the unicorn's bland appetite
the jeers of birds did disenchant her,
and straddling the bronco she loped home.

53

Cowardice

The amputated human hearts pulse in the great glass jars.
As moist and wincing red as pigeon feet, the breathing hearts
Oscillate endlessly in fluid ambiguity,
and isolated, pickle in the brine of phantasy.

The jars will never be unsealed, nor can the heart be joined,
healed, to the breast. For in that vacuum, that fatal void
between the unreal and the real, between the brine and breast
the heart will burst. And we, compassionate, cannot redeem
the prisoned hearts, nor save the crippled men, the fear-
    oppressed,
who only suffer love within the prism of a dream.

The Panic Vine

The panic vine quickens on the spine with the rise
and fall of every breath; and blooms inside the eyes.
A cold fruit bulges from the veins of wrists and arms
to bleed a virus juice into our sueded palms.
We spread disease when our be-gloved infrequent rites
of greeting are performed. If we exhume the roots
that lie in nightsoil bedded with the lungs of crows
roots watered by the coiled insistent garden hose
cold-framed against the thorn the analytic wind
the dazzling showers of the thundering sun bird blood
the grey goose feather and the white mare-mother's cud
if we expose these roots to weather and to wound
they would survive and we could bear the scattered rose
the spattered foal the honking flight and the sun's alms.

Summer Remembered

Sounds sum and summon the remembering of summers.
The humming of the sun
The mumbling in the honey-suckle vine
The whirring in the clovered grass
The pizzicato plinkle of ice in an auburn
uncle's amber glass.
The whing of father's racquet and the whack
of brother's bat on cousin's ball
and calling voices call-
ing voices spilling voices . . .

The munching of saltwater at the splintered dock
The slap and slop of waves on little sloops
The quarrelling of oarlocks hours across the bay
The canvas sails that bleat as they
are blown. The heaving buoy bell-
ing HERE I am
HERE you are HEAR HEAR

listen listen listen
The gramophone is wound
the music goes round and around
BYE BYE BLUES   LINDY'S COMING
voices calling calling calling
"Children! Children! Time's Up
Time's Up"

Merrily sturdily wantonly the familial voices
cheerily chidingly call to the children TIME'S UP
and the mute children's unvoiced clamor sacks the summer air
crying Mother Mother are you there?

Nightmare

A sleeping woman dreams she wakes
Into a surging room of shrieks
and shapes. In the frantic room a red
haired woman looms . . . on her bent arm
there sleeps a girl's carved wooden head
A doll-sized nursing bottle nipples her huge palm
Both head and bottle drop and leeringly she
beckons. The dreamer screams her hatred
of the leering shape. Scrabbling for safety
the dreamer flounders on the floor.
The leerer pounces from behind the door.
The struggling dreamer stands
The dreamer lifts and clenches both her hands
The dreamer rips the red curls
in handfuls from that hateful head and hurls
the hairy gobbets at those manic eyes
The leerer dreadfully diminishes in size
She shrinks and shrinks into a little child.
The screaming dreamer beats the dwindling child.
The dreamer lifts a chair to smash that leering child.
Nothing at all remains. Not hag nor child.
No traces and no tokens.
The red-haired dreamer wakens.

The Minotaur

The labyrinthine forest's spoor
lead to the patient Minotaur
Deep in the dark and structured core
the bull-man waits inside the maze
and he who dares explore will raze
the beast of fear behind the door.

No Ariadne and no crone
will point the way. Each man alone
must thread his path, unreel his own
life spool and fumble to the lair.
Each man must journey naked there
nor arm himself with wing nor stone.

For he who goes his armor shed
and walks with all that once he fled
that man will face the hornèd head
the unimaginable eyes
and find there where the monster dies
the ichor that the terror bled.

V

FOR MY PARENTS

"Believe in the simple magic of life, in service in the universe, and the meaning of that alertness, that 'craning of the neck' in creatures will dawn upon you."

MARTIN BUBER

That "Craning of the Neck"

The primary word is I-Thou. The primary word
I-Thou can only be spoken with the whole being. The
primary word I-It can never be spoken with the whole
being. MARTIN BUBER

Birthdays from the ocean one desert april noon
I rode through the untouching and no-odored air
astride an english saddle on a western mare
through the resisting tow-colored grass and the dune-
less sand. Under me swam a stream strange in that dried
country. A "great blue heron" stood still in the tide-
less water and when I saw him there my heart dazzled. I whispered the mare to move quietly as
Indians move, I reined her with a catpaw hand
and my breathless feet crouched into the stirrups and
I prayed her through cactus mesquite and cattlebones
to the water's edge where the tall bird fished the stones.
The listening heron expanded with despair
unloosed unwilling wings, heaved from water into air.
O he hated to fly he flapped with a splayed pain-
ful motion. Deliberate as a weathervane
he plodded through the air that touched the fishful water.
I followed him silently giving no quarter
all that afternoon. He never flew far from me
we kept meeting past each cape and estuary
but he always heaved doggedly out of touch. I
only wanted to stare myself into him to try
and thou him till we recognized and became each
other. We were both fishing. But I could not reach
his eye. He fled in puzzled ponderous pain

and I last rode home, conspicuous as Cain,
yet ashamed of a resigned demeaning pity
that denied us both. I returned to the city
and visited the zoo, fished on a concrete shore,
took children to aquariums, and rode no more.

I found that the encyclopedia says "A
gregarious bird . . ." No one spoke that desert day,
not one word. That fisher who heaved to dodge my eye
has damned himself an It and I shall never fly.

It Rained Last Night

"Nous n'irons plus aux bois,
les lauriers sont coupées."

Glass ponds astound the juicy grass, the air is wild
with the scents of thyme and fern and briny childhood
and the glistening birds call clearly in rinsed voices,
the sky is far and blue as a mariner's eye:
Listen, the greenness whistles . . .

O morning startling still and secret as a child,
a blue egg, as a moccasin in the wildwood —
O early day moving to afternoons of choices
I shall go once more to these woods until I die.
I know that the laurels grow.

West of Childhood

FOR MY BROTHER, GEORGE GARDNER

West of our childhood rote usurps the rites of spring, the wild
    sweet
season is an act of year. Uniformed robins hop and tweet
in chorus and culls from showgirls of seed catalogues doll up
    the view,
embellishing our Garden Homes, while Latin shrubs perform on
    cue.

    A child's fierce focused gaze can wholly enter
    and instantly become the bold gold center
    of a single crocus, a listening child is fused to the sole voice
    of that particular inimitable bird whose red choice
    breast is robiner than never, a child perceives
    the slow resolving of the one bud to the very leaf of leaves.

East of now and years from Illinois the shout of spring out-rang
    the dinner bell.
Brother do you remember the walled garden, our dallies in that
    ding dong dell
where my fistful of violets mazed the air we moved through and
    upon
and a swallow of brook skimmed your tabloid sloop to sea and
    gone?
North of tomorrow your daughter's daughter's ears will ding
    with spring, wild

violets will forest in her fist scenting towns of space; and my
   son's child
(weddings from this suburb) will, with crocus eyes, flower
   other Mays:
*That bud will leaf again, that choice bird sing, and paper boats
   sail down the robin days.*

Summers Ago

FOR EDITH SITWELL

The ferryman fairied us out to sea
Gold gold gold sang the apple-tree

Children I told you I tell you our sun was a hail of gold!
I say that sun stoned, that sun stormed our tranquil, our blue
  bay
bellsweet saltfresh water (bluer than tongue-can-tell, daughter)
and dazed us, darlings, and dazzled us, I say that sun crazed
(that sun clove) our serene as ceramic selves and our noon-
  glazed cove,
and children all that grew wild by the wonderful water shot tall
as tomorrow, reeds suddenly shockingly green had sprouted like
  sorrow
and crimson explosions of roses arose in that flurry of Danaean
  glory
while at night we did swoon ah we swanned to a silverer moon-
  light than listen or lute,
we trysted in gondolas blown from glass and kissed in fluted
  Venetian bliss.

Sister and brother I your mother
Once was a girl in skirling weather
Though summer and swan must alter, falter,
I waltzed on the water once, son and daughter.

68

Canzonetta

FOR A GOD-SON AGED FIVE,
STEWART GARDNER

Swim little king-fish   Leap small salmon
Sally from the sea and up the stream   Fling
Game as Isaac and gold as Mammon
Plunge April fishlet Sprintheart dash
Drought's the drowning though love is rash
And Anglers bait to poach your dreaming
   Cheat that larder, Beat that Chowder, Splash!

Gambol Gamble Easter lambling
Adam as Ram and mortal as Mother
Baa your benison   Ding your damning
Bruise and blessing bell your bleating
Carillon lambkin rousting routing no retreating
Hurtle into wolf and spring's bell-wether
   Spiel your glock and,   spell your flock, and   Ring!

Gallivant giddyap bantam Will-joy
Bold as bugle and brave as bunting
Trumpet! Furl out! Bannering boy
Gallop to the hill-top. Strut your stride
Raising praising choosing losing never hide-
ing, heeled by the hope that hounds your hunting
   Sound your horn   Astound your dawn and   Ride

Children are Game

I have come often to this forest,
home to these never not green trees.
Now, in a grove of auburn bones
the spindling skeletons of summer flowers,
I hear the soft snow hiss through fir and spruce,
the shrill quick children skating on the pond
a safe and thousand miles from reef and shark.
What wings will whistle down this resined bark,
what monstrous blooming blast belief?
Children should not come to grief.
I swore that even crows could sing
I thawed my winters thinking spring
and now am always cold, with reason,
for bombs can blossom any season.
The pheasant's chicks scratch posted ground,
children are game the whole year round
skating the thin ice of the pond
gay and innocent and spruce:
while I in a grave of once-were flowers
and stiffer than their thready bones
forget these seen to be green trees
too mindful of the forest.

Fall in Massachusetts

I saw the tall bush burn.
(Nineteen times a gallows-tree . . .
The tongue of fire muted by our guilt. There cannot be
a voice for deaf New Englanders vowed never to be healed.)
I saw where a manna of flame had unfallowed the starving field
          where a witch charred
          where her bones roared
where each of the good-wives took her choice of holiday or
     skewered house
and the mewing children barked another name
to their elders gathering apple-wood boughs
          and the sweet, the kindling fern:
          while cinders blew; and shame.

Little Rock Arkansas 1957

DEDICATED TO THE NINE CHILDREN

Clasping like bucklers to their bodies, books,
nine children move through blasts of killing looks.
Committed to this battle each child dares,
deliberately, the fusillades of jeers.
Their valor iron in their ironed clothes
they walk politely in their polished shoes
down ambushed halls to classrooms sown with mines
to learn their lesson. Obviously nine's
a carefully calculated number, odd
not even, a suave size that can be add-
ed to, discreetly, later, or culled now
should one child break not bend; or fail to bow
sufficiently his bloody head . . . a rule
to heed, child, be you brave and going to school.

A Loud Song, Mother

FOR MY SON, DANIEL SEYMOUR

My son is five years old and tonight he sang this song to me.
He said, it's a loud song, Mother, block up your ears a little, he
said wait I must get my voice ready first. Then tunelessly
but with a bursting beat he chanted from his room enormously,
        strangers in my name
        strangers all around me
        strangers running toward me
        strangers all over the world
        strangers running on stars
A deafening declaration this jubilant shout of grief
that trumpets final fellowship and flutes a whole belief.
Alone and in the dark he clears his throat to yawp his truth
that each living human creature's name is Ruth.
He sings a world of strangers running on the burning stars
a race on every-colored feet with freshly calloused scars.

Our stark still strangers waited back of doors and under beds
their socket eyes stared at us out of closets; in our heads.
We crawled on hob-nailed knees across our wasted starless land
each smugly thinking his the only face that wore a brand.
Sons, may you starve the maggot fears that ate our spirit's meat
and stride with brother strangers in your seven-league bare feet.

VI

Animula vagula blandula
Hospes comesque corporis
Quae nunc abibis in loca
Pallidula rigida nudula

HADRIAN TO HIS SOUL

Timeo

Dear God (safe ambiguity)
If I address you faithlessly
The fear of heaven devils me.
Could I be sure of purgatory
Sure I could praise and not adore thee
I might a tepid faith embrace.
But I am terrified of grace.
Gethsemane is any place.

Not at All What One Is Used To . . .

There was never any worry about bread or even butter
although that worried me almost as much as my stutter.
I drank coffee with the others in drugstores and then went
back to my room for which I paid a lower rent
than I could afford and where I was proud
of the bedbugs, and where I often allowed
myself an inadequate little Rhine wine. Two
or three times a week after seeing the producers who
were said to be looking for comedy types I wandered
off to the movies alone and always wondered
if anyone in the mezzanine knew me by sight, or might
know me by name or have kissed me and I felt an itch
to stand right up and ask, like swearing out loud in church.
Only one agent agreed to be rude to me every day, a
cross cockeyed woman who had acted in her youth.
I was not union because I had never been paid and the truth
is no other agent would speak to me or even see me until I was
        Equity . . .
a vicious circle but not unpleasing to me.
I smoked for hours in producers' anterooms where
I prayed that interviews I had come there
to beseech would be denied.
Usually my prayers were granted and I stayed outside.
I was a tense impostor, a deliberate dunce,
in a lobby of honest earnest seekers. Once
or twice thanks to a letter of introduction I

got to see the man, but instead of "chin up" and "do or die"
I effectively slouched and stammered in disorder in order
to thus escape the chance to read I might be
offered. An English director once said I was the
"perfect adorable silly ass," due in part to a part
he saw me do in which I had to lisp and giggle.
But that of course was in another country. I did not boggle
at summer stock and somewhere north of Boston I had
at last become a paid member of a company where sad
to relate I was successfully grotesque in numerous unglamorous
bit parts (usually dialect for I did not stutter
in dialect) and I was always differently grotesque, utter-
ly; but people laughed and/or cried, always saying I was playing myself, that I was a "natural." Through the good offices
        of a
well-connected friend I at last read for a producer who was
        Broadway
and was given the part of a Cockney maid, afraid
and eager, who moved and talked in double-time.
But I was fired. The stars complained for no rime
or reason that they became confused when I was "on" (there
        was no basis
for their saying that the audience laughed too much and in the
        wrong places)
although it is possible that I just did everything faster and faster
I had come to depend on the laughs and dismissal was a disaster.
My next job was a haughty lady's maid with a faint brogue
and a strip-tease walk. One night (in Hartford) I was more
        rogue-
ish than usual and the college boys broke up the show
banging their feet on the floor and whistling. Not long ago

I portrayed a madwoman (but gentle and sentimental)
I curtseyed, sang a short song as I did not
stammer when I sang, and fondled a telescope that
had belonged to a sea-going ancestor. It was agreed
that at last, despite previous successes, I had indeed
and finally found my niche. It was declared
that I could go on and on doing that kind of thing, but I dared
myself to attempt only straight parts although it is hard (playing
    with fire)
for a character actress to play herself and only too true
that the audience response is not at all what one is used to.
Nevertheless it is a challenge and no reason to retire.

Writing Poetry

is one game that no-one quits while he or she's ahead. The
stakes are steep. Among the chips are love fame life and sanity.
The game's risk is that winning one chip often means the forfeit
of another but despite the penalties there is a surfeit
of players. Some are only kibbitzers, others play it safe
(their chips are counterfeit) cheating, they may not come to
    grief,
or so they hope, and hoping keep their places near the pot.
There are other gambits deployed to trick the croupier's hot
eye and hand. For some in terror for their reason and their
    rhyme
there's a disguise in style to rent or borrow or assume:
hair-shirts, brocaded waistcoats (the gilt is slightly tarnished)
sackcloth interlined, embroidered chasubles refurbished,
helmets turbans caps (with bells) wreaths high silk hats cock-
    ades . . .
and for women Quaker bonnets wimples coifs and sun-shades,
long blue stockings hawking gloves a fan a hobnailed boot.
But it's the gamblers wearing their own hides who shoot
the moon rocketing on unprotected feet to outer space
where (out of pocket, having no sleeves up which to hide an
    ace)
they fall bankrupt or being down to their last chip are stran-
ded. No-one has pocketed the moon since the game began . . .
or . . . sooner than they did
they died.

When a Warlock Dies

FOR DYLAN THOMAS

When a warlock dies his rout of lemans, demons, fallen angels
and Familiars bend to the brewing of elegiac potions, fruity
    runes
plummed with their dead's distinctive spells,
mournful marketable meads composted of his rich remains.

As an apprentice witch, a mere familiar of Familiars, my
sunday-go-to-funeral broomstick (wreathed with mistletoe)
is handy to bestride in a cortège, to stir the baked meats, or to
    fly
a'wake-ing. Surely this deft-dirged, over-o-
ded, buzzard-hungry, heron-lonely, phoenix-hearted, gull-lunged
hummingbird-pulsed, falcon-winged and lark-tongued
Chanticleer has crowed his own Farewells and Hails.
And not all the ink and drink and spunk from Wichita to Wales
will wake this cock. The homage of our elegies whistles against
    the night
that looms too close for comfort since his death and our uncom-
    fortable respite.

The roaring riming of this most mourned Merlin canticles his
    praise and His, and ours,
and Jerichos the walls of heaven with a surfing shout of love,
    and blasts of flowers.

"... And Thou No Breath at All?"

FOR BARBARA RANSOM JOPSON, 1915–1957

Yours, Barbara, was a literal way of death.
You were defaulted by the failure of your breath.
To fox the taxing of your faltering breath
you schooled yourself for years to snare
a reasonable surety of air . . .
not surplus air to waltz or to embrace
just marginal sips to stay, with grace,
alight, and spark the hovering dark of death
with bright unwavering speech. You flogged your breath
down your dogged days and spent that wilting breath
in dialogues that burnished us with your
ungarnishable gold where we before
had counterfeited in our brass or gilt. Your art
was alchemy wrought by a sleight of heart.
That art will lend us gold beyond your death
and round the bend of our last breath
when we like you end, as we must, all out of breath.

Zei Gesund*

FOR DR. LOUIS CHOLDEN, 1918–1956

In the preposterous sunlight
we watched them wincingly lower you
into your formal April grave.
In strict tears they tolled the Hebrew
litanies which (though you were not pious)
had wailed in the ark of your ear
and blown in the shule of your heart
as remindingly as Shofar.
You lived your life and died your death by
love, and if on that spring day you could
have spoken from the upholstered
isolation of your coffin, you would
have taken to yourself the sorrow
of your uncountable bereaved,
as you did always, possibly saying "that
I am the reason you are grieved
and that I cannot rouse to laugh you out
of tears distresses me as dying
can no longer." Louis, it is true
that when those loved do die our crying
is made most difficult to suffer
by the unstoppable sharing

Zei Gesund is a Yiddish phrase meaning literally
"Be Well"; it is used in leave-taking; therefore: "Farewell." *Shule* is the Jewish word for temple; *shofar*, for
the ram's horn blown on the Day of Judgment.

of what we imagine to have been
the die-er's panic and despairing
in this ultimate encounter.
You spared us that pain, for knowing
your life-spirit robust past compare
we knew that you had braved your going
with your accustomed curiosity
and calm and courage. Every tear
is for ourselves, for our own loss,
the forever absence of you. Were
Death a hag (like those dishevelled
ladies in asylums whom you re-
deemed to dignity through your
accepting word and touch) I do believe you would have lent Ma Death a
comb for her lank locks and would fear-
lessly have stroked her fleshless shoulder
saying gently "Why Mrs. Bones, my dear,
haven't you come a little early?"
I think you would not have withheld
even from Death's self your thou-ing
greeting once you beheld
that Incurable at your elbow.
You fought to keep her waiting for
you in the hallway while she
scratched and finally pounded on your door
but once she entered and that door closed
behind her you recognized the fact
of her outrageous presence and the
courtesy and courage of your heart listened intact
to her untimely undeniable demand.

It is not easy to remember that you died.
Neither your funeral nor our tears persuade
us, yet, that you have died. We shall confide
to you in phantasy through years of need
the flabby failure, shabby sin, and pride-
fully, the high Hungarian deed.
Our spirits shall by your quick soul be fed
until our bodies, too, are dead.

In Memory of Lemuel Ayers, Scene Designer,
Dead of Cancer in His Fortieth Year

It is generall
To be mortall
I have well espied
No man may him hide
from death hollow-eyed.
JOHN SKELTON

I that indulgently
am still allowed to be
address these lines to the
"Late Lemuel Ayers" who
did not elect to do
his dying young

Lem you are early late
your life and death complete,
somewhere our dyings wait.
Finished with and by pain
you will not feel again
forgive us grief

Magical from the start
your strict and dazzling art
pure as your eye's taut heart
delicate bold and rare
castled the empty air
splendoring space

Truth-vizored knight of risk
vulnerable in your casque
magician of the masque
sword-want in hand you strove
to conquer goat-foot's grove,
laurel your crown

Raped of felicity
ambushed unknowingly
by your bones' treachery
outraged by cone and knife
you labored for your life,
Myrtle, your wreath

Now you indulgently
observe our boon to be
alive and grieved, but the
shame is you've few friends who
dare to expect to do
their dying old.

Homo Gratia Artis

Ass-eared cross-gartered haloed crowned
Pearl-eyed and coral-boned and drowned
Victim-father son bride-mother
You are Abel and his brother
Eden Persepolis and Hell
Raskolnikoff and Philomel
The lamb the unicorn the goat
The burning shirt and Joseph's coat
The bleeding ear the bled-for nose
The apple mistletoe and rose
You are the coffin and the cock
The pain the talon and the rock.

This Room Is Full of Clocks

I am trying to write at a desk that is mine
these mornings thanks to the kindness of a stranger.
His room is full of clocks. All of them are ticking.
I fumble through a folder of abandoned poems
and of news stories I cut from papers I must
have conned some enterprising morning years ago.

Here is the account of a rare black swan that flew
from somewhere to Waukegan Harbor to a Greek
café where "it huddled at the door its feathers
drenched with oil." The swan was sad reports the paper, so
    Mathon
Kyritsis, restaurant keeper and fisherman,
consulted an ornithologist who said the
sorry bird was one of one hundred nineteen Black
Australian Swans that still survive and that the bird
could not live in captivity without its mate.
No doubt this Rare Swan died of fatigue let alone
bereavement even before I snipped the clippings.
Perhaps Mr. Kyritsis lives telling his tale . . .
The paper did not give the age of Mathon K.

Here's a clipping with the heading ANIMALS:
HOW OLD THEY GET. It is an accounting from "the
reliable records of zoos, aquariums

and aviaries all over the world," offered
with comments by the Cook County Forest Preserve.
For instance it says here that "man is longer lived
than any other mammal," and sure enough the
record shows a pampered elephant only made
it to sixty-nine. It is different for some
of our poets. MacNeice and Roethke have died
at fifty-five just like the Giant Salamander
while an occasional catfish is alive at
sixty. I don't begrudge the turkey-buzzard his
one hundred and eighteen years, nor the swan who if
he has his mate can live to one hundred and two
(that rare Black Swan who flew to Waukegan did not)
but I mind reading that coddled alligators
(safe from such random killers as love or neglect)
are able to thrash and lash and grin at sixty-eight.
Even in these days not Thomas, Cummings, Roethke
or MacNeice have managed that. It is possible
that there should be a Forest Preserve for poets
each with his or her mate but I remind myself
that the poet is rumoured to be less constant
than the swan. No the bard must do his best with book
and bed and booze and blunders of the heart and
bearing witness burying friends banning bombs
and using onomatopeia with restraint.

A Word from the Piazza Del Limbo

Infrequently but massively I hear
from one who until recently seemed crammed
with *caritas*. Now, since the saving of his
soul his letters speak only of himself and
of Him and of their correspondence.
Indeed he declines to address himself to my
distress. Although I have written him of
various despairs he does not even
upbraid me for Sloth, the sin with which
I wake and eat, that monkey on my back.
I realize that right this minute he may
be praying for me (though fretfully, the
way one writes a postponed letter, I MUST
pray for Belle today) because being yet
but a fresh-washed lamb he is bound to be
nervous about wasting God's time, and of
course his own which I can well understand.
I can also see that he has his own
chores if only, for Heaven's sake, keeping in
good with God, with whom he has a close but
complicated relationship, while I at present
lack even a genuflecting acquaintance.
Not God's fault God knows. I have avoided
Him since losing innocence. I do not
say evaded because though arrogant,
I cannot imagine that He has been

loping breathlessly after me all these
years hoping to heal me and herd me to
the fold. When I was a clear-eyed child,
reading about Artemis and Snow White,
I secretly got down on my knees when
the light clicked out and my brother and I
had said our I Lay Me's and been kissed.
We slept on a screened porch almost out of
doors. In winter the bare floor was arctic
and I made certain that my knees were bare.
Then (a confirmed believer in my own
omnipotence) I prayed and prayed
for the maimed the halt the blind, the hungry,
for every category of misery
that I could, in innocence, imagine.
No syllable of my petition ever varied
lest that deflect my power to persuade.
Yes, I was magical then. I could fly.
When I climbed a tree I put my arms round
the trunk and my ear to the bark and heard,
faintly, the dryad speaking, and I had the evil eye;
and the Unicorn's head once lay in my lap, and bareback
I galloped Pegasus. I moved Mt. Monadnock.
I walked across blue Mt. Hope Bay. I believed.

I lived too long a time in innocence,
but not quite long enough to wholly make break or addle
me. A critic wrote "the pilgrim for whom no chapel
waits." But still I wear the scallop shell
and shall till I go down the well
            Ding   Dong   Belle

M